CONSTANT COMPANION

Mary Susan Spencer Cuminale

ISBN 979-8-89428-433-0 (paperback)
ISBN 979-8-89428-434-7 (hardcover)
ISBN 979-8-89428-435-4 (digital)

Copyright © 2024 by Mary Susan Spencer Cuminale

All rights reserved. No part of this publication may be reproduced, distributed, or transmitted in any form or by any means, including photocopying, recording, or other electronic or mechanical methods without the prior written permission of the publisher. For permission requests, solicit the publisher via the address below.

Christian Faith Publishing
832 Park Avenue
Meadville, PA 16335
www.christianfaithpublishing.com

Printed in the United States of America

November 5, 2023

Set the clocks back one hour. Do the people responsible know the havoc they cause by taking away an hour of daylight?

November 7, 2023

I'm sitting in my brown polyester recliner in my bedroom (previously known as the cell for a year and four months). But that is another story. I sat there letting my mind wander and said to myself, *It is so dark, cold, gloomy this time of year. I wish I could go somewhere sunny and warm, but where? Whom could I visit? Would anyone want to go with me?* Blank…blank…blank. Ah, my bucket list popped into my mind. Ever since COVID-19, when I pursued my family heritage, I had this burning desire to find the church my twenty-third great-grandfather built in the year 1256 in a place called Swallowfield, United Kingdom. Ah, but it's dark, cold, gloomy this time of year there too! Prayed. Prayed hard asking for an answer. It came to me to pick up my cell phone and entered "flights to London."

There staring back at me was a flight from Rochester to Charlotte, North Carolina, and on to London Heathrow. Wait for it…$532 *round trip*! Booked it for November 12 and return November 28, 2023. Four days to plan and pack, and yes, I'm going with God.

November 12, 2023; arrival, November 13, 2023
Sunday into Monday

I have no fear. Quite the opposite. I am full of excitement, anticipation, and joy. I'm so glad to be getting out of Dodge, as they say, and leave all the heartache it's held over my life behind for a desperately needed refresher course. Of course, heartache travels silently in the passenger seat, but then God rested within.

The flight was uneventful, just the way I like them. I had booked a Jay Ride Taxi to pick me up at Heathrow Airport with the sign saying MARY SUSAN CUMINALE to take me directly to the Mill House Inn in Swallowfield, United Kingdom. I had never been privileged to see my name on a card at an airport or have a limo driver take my luggage and direct me. I wasn't this time either. I waited, and I called the company, and the bottom line was they could not find the reservation. Now what? *It's going to be alright*, I told myself. I went to the currency exchange to get some pounds for travel and met a wonderful man from India who saw and heard my dilemma.

"No worries," he said. "This is easy. You take the train, only one change in between and then Reading. You can take a taxi from there to the Inn in Swallowfield."

Thank God I have learned to pack light over the years. I had my small roller black-and-white polka-dot carry-on and a matching shoulder bag. Follow the signs, follow the signs, follow the signs. Ask questions. Up and down escalators. In and out of trains, the tube, turnstiles, tickets purchased, and slid into proper corridors, and Reading, England, was achieved!

I walked outside and breathed in the delicious fresh air and sunshine for the first time in twenty-four hours. And there directly in front of me was one, just one black cab (like the ones you see in all the black-and-white British movies) that took me directly to the Inn. I was given a cup of tea and hugs from the staff upon arrival once they discovered I was from America to see the church in their little town. Did I die and come to heaven? I was excited to tell how I came upon my information during COVID-19 on MyHeritage.Com, and from that moment on, I was family.

After settling into my room upstairs and viewing my surroundings out the back window, I started to cry. How could I be this bold to come to an unknown area by myself? Ah, it was getting dark, and I was starving and in search of a good glass of wine and some dinner. I ate in the dining room alone in silence, sipping a delectable glass of burgundy from France and caught my breath. I ordered bangers and mash. This is a typical common folk dish that I have had in the past and wasn't particularly fond of or did I crave. Yet it was ordered for old times' sake, and I cannot begin to tell you the delectable smell that wafted into my senses when it was served. The first bite into my mouth was utterly outstanding, and I devoured every bite of two English sausages and mashed potatoes with gravy. Time to rest. Happy birthday, my darling daughter. Thank You, Lord, for this day.

November 14, 2023
Tuesday

I woke early, refreshed and excited to start my new day. I made myself a cup of tea in my room, still pinching myself that I indeed was in Swallowfield, England.

This trip has been on my bucket list since COVID-19 hit the world, and I was pretty much stuck inside my home with not much to accomplish. This was not me. I must be doing something productive every day, if possible, even if it is mundane tasks. Helping others brings me joy at my core; it's what keeps me motivated to "carry on and mind your step" or "mind your head." These signs are everywhere. Very British! So I freshened up with a shower this time. Last night I took a bath in the typical very narrow bathtub and nearly had to remain there. To say it's a trick to maneuver the British bathing is an understatement. Use your imagination. Now I am ready for coffee and a full British breakfast.

I was greeted warmly in the dining room. Everyone was kind to ask if I had slept well and if there was anything I needed. Breakfast served of two sunny-side-up fried eggs from the owners' farm, a rasher of bacon (two slices, more like Canadian), fried mushrooms, fried half of tomato, and, yes, fried potatoes. Homemade toast and strawberry jam completed my outstanding, very filling meal. Everyone in the hotel knew by this time my reason for coming to the Swallowfield Inn and wanted to know how they could help. I merely needed to know the direction of the church as I was ready to walk.

It's a beautiful day, sunny and warm for November, 55°F. Out the door I went, crossed the road, minding my step. I walked on the left side, which was extremely narrow, two and a half feet at best with a tall hedgerow approximately six feet on my left. The first car came whizzing past me, and I believe if I stuck my right arm out straight, it would be gone. I didn't stick my arm out. After a mile or so, I approached a building that looked like a vicarage, and it had numerous cars in the parking lot. I approached a window where I saw someone inside.

This woman, now known as Vicky, opened the door and said in her totally wonderful British accent, "Oh, hello, may I help you?"

I said, "I hope so. I'd like to see the Swallowfield church that my twenty-third great-grandfather Sir John de Spencer built in 1256, if possible."

Her look was priceless as she said, "Do come in."

The questions began: where was I from, why, and what. Vicky now stated, "I am the church historian! And, of course, I have the key."

We talked for over an hour and became friends. She had plans after work but then offered to pick me up at the Swallowfield Inn tomorrow morning, as I hadn't rented a car, and take me to the church. I was so excited. I walked back to the inn and had a cup of tea and a biscuit (cookie), kicked my feet up, and went sound asleep. I don't adhere to jet lag; however, I freshened for dinner and went downstairs.

Quiet, very quiet. I rang the little bar bell, and Jason came. He poured me a glass of the fabulous burgundy from France I had the night before. In walked a gentleman who was introduced to me as Jurij from Lithuania. He worked fairly nearby and occasionally stayed when he had long days at the office rather than traveling back home. He joined into the conversation we were having about AI, and after twenty minutes or so, he said, "Would you join me for dinner?"

"Um, sure. Who wouldn't say yes to a tall, handsome, intelligent man?"

We sat in the dining room where there were a few more patrons enjoying the atmosphere and a meal. The conversation continued along with a wonderful meal for two hours. We prayed together, cried together, laughed like two crazy people, and took a selfie to forever remember the chance meeting of two strangers now friends. What a wonderful day 2. Thank You, Lord.

November 15, 2023
Wednesday

I had another great night of blissful sleep in a king-size bed from heaven. I was wide awake and dressed and ready to go downstairs for another full British breakfast. Repeat deliciousness! Vicky picked me up at 9:00 a.m. as previously arranged, and off we went to All Saints Church.

I had to catch my breath when we approached the gates. Was I really here fulfilling my dream? I walked through the graveyard not knowing if any Spencer relatives were buried there.

I know Vicky was talking, but I honestly didn't hear her. I was in my own world. I took a few pictures so I could relive this experience later. Vicky was patiently waiting at the door. *The Normandy door* from 1120!

The key was immense and was turned to open the church. I stepped in, and it literally took my breath away. I was gasping, trying to take in my first view.

This was far beyond my comprehension to grasp. I had imagined a decrepit, dusty, dark, musty, creepy space. Instead, it was a space of bright, spacious lofty design, fresh, clean, and so welcoming. Original beams caught my eye that were hand-hewed from local trees from the nearby forest of so long ago and were in sturdy condition. This is an example of late medieval "scissor-bracing" of bell turret. Now to the stained glass windows also preserved. Stunning doesn't explain the beauty of the morning sun blazing through them; perhaps radiantly glorious is a better description.

The east window was restored in 1870. So here is the history of the church as documented. My great-grandfather John de Spencer was the son of Galfridus LeSpencer and Emma DeHarcourt. She was a close friend of King Henry III and Queen Eleanor. John married Joan de Lou, and they lived at Swallowfield Park. John wrote the then pope Alexander IV and requested permission to build the church, stating it was far too dangerous to go to mass in Shinfield because of the dangers from robbers in the summer through the Windsor Woods and floods in the winter from the Loddon River. The river runs next to the inn. The pope granted permission, and when the church was completed, he sent a bishop to officiate mass.

After a two-hour visit at the church in which I got to know more about Vicky, I was invited to come to "a coffee run." I said yes without knowing what a coffee run was. I wrongly presumed it was getting a coffee and running with it! I was wrong. We went back to the vicarage, and I met a good group of seven gentlemen and eleven ladies of the church. They do this weekly. The men bring their old heritage cars, tops off (the cars, not the men), and boast or chat about the next road adventure. Generally, the ladies make cakes and other treats and serve coffee or tea. It is strictly volunteer, and they take turns being the server, washing up, etc. One pound is charged per slice of cake, and all the funds go to assisting the church with flowers for Sunday service. Poppies were the theme this week, remembering WWII veterans. Did I mention they hold service every Sunday these days?

Currently sixty persons are listed as parishioners, and twenty-five or so are consistent Sunday worshippers. Can I say incredible one more time? One of the ladies invited me to her home for cocktails the next night. Another stated, "Oh, we could go to the pub after for dinner!" I said I would be honored. More to follow tomorrow.

Then I walked back to the inn for a quick rest. Afterward, I took another walk out to the left this time. Sidenote: the dangerous woods were later named Spencerswood, and the tiny village is on the edge of the former dense woods.

Blink, and you've gone through it. A pub, a bakery, a petrol station, nail and hair salon, and many homes that are in impeccable condition are there. Crazy Brits walking in shorts. It was pouring rain, and I had on my brand-new trainers and an umbrella, which did no good whatsoever. Walking along the road for a bit more than a mile one way, I was soaked literally to the bone through my jacket. I did stop to take pictures of a beautiful white stallion who seemed as happy to see me as I was to see him. He kept neighing and pacing back and forth along this fence. I took his picture. Never mind, I got treats in the bakery that I had later in the day.

Back to John, he was knighted in 1256 (now Sir John) at the age of twenty-one and built the church in the same year. He died at age thirty-nine in 1274 and was buried in the church grounds. During the 1871 restoration, his stone tomb was found buried under the front door. An alcove under the west window was restored and now housed his stone sarcophagus. I touched it and cried.

The name of his church is All Saints Church. Meticulous care has been taken over the years to preserve this church—credited to the residents of a very small quaint town called Swallowfield five miles from Reading, thirty-eight miles from London.

The only street is called the Street. Clever.

Once back at the inn, I stripped out of my soggy clothes and took a shower and a nap after my tart and tea. Dinner was delicious, and I had another glass of French wine. Then I caught up with current bad news on the tele and went off to sleep. Fifteen thousand steps today. Thank You, Lord, for another brilliant day.

November 16, 2023
Thursday

    I took another walk to Spencerswood today as the sun was shining, and I really didn't have anything going until tonight. Just before I left when I went downstairs, to my surprise, there were the seven men from the coffee run! I discovered they get together every Thursday at the inn to converse. I took a great picture of them along with the owner of the inn. Turned out he owned the horse farm! A similar walk but so much nicer in sunshine. Mr. White Horse was not there again.

    I stopped in the bakery and got a pastry for lunch as I didn't indulge in another full breakfast today. Today was restful, but I still walked ten thousand steps. Vicky picked me up, and we went to Margaret's home. It was so warm and inviting. We were six including me and were served wine and hors d'oeuvres along with great conversations and lots of questions to me and so many laughs. The biggest two questions were, Why and how do I travel alone? My reply, "I'm never alone!"

    After an hour or so, we went to the pub—across The Street. I had fish and chips and a beer, and it was brill! I got to meet several more people, including the owner. These are keeper friends now. I hate to leave, but I must.

    I slept like a stone. Thank You, Lord, for another memory-filled day full of joy and love.

November 17, 2023
Friday

    I readied myself and packed the three outfits I now admit needed a good wash and tried to slip out early for my scheduled Uber ride to the Reading train station. I hate long goodbyes; however, it wasn't to be avoided. The entire staff including the kitchen staff came to bid me farewell and a safe journey. Hugs and kisses and prayers for your blessings, my dearest people. I have no doubt this quaint Victorian inn, which was previously a flour mill for many years before it became my welcoming abode that I have ever had the privilege to stay in. Fairtheewell, Swallowfield. I shall miss you. Till we meet again.

Now back at the train station in Reading, I had to put on my thinking cap to reverse the trip here to return to London. Two trains later with a switch in between, I arrived unscathed. Mind your step and mind your head signs in between. I then found the train to Poole Harbor and boarded. I thoroughly enjoyed all the stops that I was familiar with. Although there has never been a train stop in the New Forest, I was able to see some wild horses and deer through my window. Ah, the wonderful memories. But that's another story for another time.

I arrived at Winchester at 10:31 a.m., Southampton Central at 11:02 a.m., Bournemouth 11:53 a.m., and ending in Poole Harbor, where my friend Mandy was waiting on the platform to greet me. Her first words to me were "I have wine and sandwiches and tea. We're going to the beach hut!"

Who was I to argue? I feel like I am home. I lived in Canford Cliffs in 1995–1996 and again in 2002, but those times are another story. A quick stop home to freshen up and grab the prepared dishes and wine, and down to the beach we went.

This beach was listed as the number one best beach in the United Kingdom when I first lived here.

I came to take care of a neurologist with ALS from the University of Rochester, New York. His name was Dr. David M. Marsh, and he grew up in the area. That, my dear readers, is a total book all by itself. The Brits were running along the promenade in their shorts like it was a summer day instead of in the fifties. A few brave hearts went for a dip in the sea, laughing and enjoying themselves immensely. Many were throwing sticks for their dogs to chase and bring back. It always amazed me how well-behaved dogs are everywhere I go. They are welcome in the best of restaurants throughout the country, beach paws and all. They can be found lying underneath many a table in the pubs.

We stayed only a couple hours because Mandy invited an old dear friend of mine, Lilly, to join us for dinner at her home. Mandy had another friend staying with her at the weekend who was observing a class at Bournemouth University, overseeing a project. She has lived all over the world: Singapore, Dubai, the list was endless. I enjoyed her quiet demeanor and graceful presence. She also participates in the practice of mindfulness. We all had an enjoyable evening reminiscing, but now it was time for some sleep in "the closet under the stairs." Literally, an army cot with space to have a table and plug in my phone, hang some of my clothes to dry after a machine wash, and a place for my suitcase. Again, I slept like a rock. Thank You, Lord, for another brilliant day!

November 18, 2023
Saturday

The three of us decided to go in to Branksome for a hearty late breakfast and some browsing in the charity shops. We were in perfect sync, laughing, telling mad crazy stories, and indulging in life. I bought a delightful owl pin for two pounds ($2.57 US) in one shop, and in another, I spied a pair of sunglasses with rhinestones in the corners, and I went mad about them; they were also two pounds. My friends said, "You like those?" And I said, "I must have them. They are fabulous darlings!" Done and done.

We tried to get into the smallest movie theater in England called Bournemouth Colosseum, but it was closed. I took a picture at least. The last stop was a French cheese shop called Renouf's Pantry. This was my treat for Mandy for being so kind. I bought several different cheeses, some Italian olives, crackers, salamis, and nuts. When we finally returned to the flat (apartment), we were all ready for some mindfulness.

Later that evening, I put together a charcuterie platter on top of field greens, and we opened some wine, and voilà, dinner was served. Ah, what a perfect end to a simply marvelous day. No television, no music, just peacefulness and insightful conversation. Thank You, Lord, once again for your abundance of blessings.

November 19, 2023
Sunday

Leisure waking—served a cup of tea just the way I like it in my cupboard. Mandy said she was minding me, and I loved it! Went to the living room and cozied up on the couch. Everyone was now on their computers. I had to figure out where I was going next. It was between Tynemouth, to research further the Heslop side of the family on my mother's side, or Devon, where the Hoppers on my father's mother's side originated. I decided on Tynemouth, near the Scottish border. With the decision made, I proceeded to book the train tickets with Mandy minding me. Done.

Now my new friend Alycia casually said, "There's a concert tonight at the Pavilion in Bournemouth. Jools Holland and his rhythm and blues orchestra with Ruby Turner and Pauline Black of the Selector (who were famous in the United Kingdom in the '80s) as the main venue."

Mandy semi-squealed, remembered the mindfulness, and then questioned the price of the tickets; it was pricey. I said, "You only go around once. I'll pay my share!" Booked and done!

Now I was minding Mandy and Lis. The girls and I got a little gussied up and sipped a glass or possibly two before the taxi picked us up. The venue called the Pavilion at Bournemouth Gardens was mobbed with people and cars, and Mandy was smart not to drive in the madness that is Bournemouth. Can I honestly tell you I have never been to a better concert in my life? I had no idea who these entertainers were, my being from the USA, but I know them now! Jools is a phenomenal piano genius who loves jazz, rhythm and blues, and the New Orleans–style honky-tonk.

After the opening group started, Smith and Brewer, and throughout their performance, the crowd was typical British. By that I mean no one was tapping their feet or hands; there wasn't even a tilt of the head. My initial thought was these people were so stoic! They listened but quietly and didn't show any outward emotion. *I had to sit on my hands and cross my legs to keep from moving!* I cried listening to one song entitled "Love You Forever." They did clap enthusiastically at the end of the performance.

During the intermission, I went into the lobby hopefully to meet them both, which I did. I told Brewer how very much their songs moved my heart and purchased two CDs. Yes, CDs. He told me they were called at the very last moment to perform as the group that was initially planned had illness. My good fortune.

Now back in our seats, the lights went up, and Jools Holland sat down at the piano, and the opening number began. It kept the Brits in their seats, but could it be their heads were moving to the beat? By the third song, toes started tapping, hands were clapping, and excitement started to fill the room. By the end of the concert, everyone was dancing. I mean everyone! *Wow*, what astonishing entertainers they all were.

Happily exhausted, we returned to the flat, had a spot of tea, and promptly went to bed as all of us had an early start the next day. Thank You, Lord, for yet another incredible day. I know how much I am blessed.

November 20, 2023
Monday

Up at 4:30 a.m. and left the flat at 5:30 a.m. Mandy dropped me off at the Poole train station for my very early train to Newcastle, England, near the Scottish border.

My final destination was Tynemouth, England, to find little Albert Edward Heslip, born 1901 in Northern Ireland. I discovered he existed when investigating my mother's side of the family on the My Heritage site during the COVID-19 pandemic in 2020. Heslip is my grandmother's maiden name. It was spelled Haslip on her marriage certificate here in the USA. However, on the 1901 Northern Ireland census, the family was listed under William Heslip, head of household, age fifty-nine, farm laborer, and my great-grandfather. Ann Jane Heslip, wife, age fifty-four (my great-grandmother); Minnie Heslip, daughter, seamstress, age eighteen (my grandmother); followed by Albert Edward Heslip, grandson, age one month, in black and white on the 1901 census form. From that moment on, he went straight to my heart, and I had to discover what happened to him (my first uncle). What was his destiny? Hence, I am on a fast train headed north where I further discovered many other Heslip members going back to the year 1570. My dearest uncle Albert Edward, I am on my way to hopefully find you.

It was a very long train ride, or should I say rides? I went direct to London station from Poole Harbor on the Southern Rail System without any difficulty, and I immensely enjoyed the scenery along the route as it was a beautiful sunny day and brought back so many memories of towns and villages I've visited back when I lived in

Canford Cliffs. The New Forest has stayed in my heart, but that's yet another story.

When I got to London Waterloo, I had to change stations and walk quite a distance, but after sitting for three hours or so, it was good to stretch my legs and move. Eventually, I found my way to the on-time train. I had a mere twenty minutes to switch railways and had to run the last five or so, yes, literally run—dragging the suitcase and shoulder bag. I hopped aboard the Northeastern Railway train, and the door shut behind me immediately, and off we went. Phew! I found my assigned seat, Coach K, seat 69, Kings Cross to Newcastle, which had a table between two double coach seats where I was able to spread out and plug in my laptop and cell phone to recharge. Two gentlemen were staring at me from across the table. I smiled, they nodded. One of them finally spoke, thank God. Otherwise, this would have been a very long three-and-a-half-hour train ride.

It turned out only one spoke some English as they were from Saudi Arabia, and Arabic was their primary language. Well, we managed to exchange niceties and laughed a lot. They were lovely gentlemen. Now along came the ticket master, and guess what…they were in the wrong car, which are alphabetical; they're meant to be in Coach C. Off they went, and the three people standing and waiting for their original assigned place scooted into their seats. Well, these three were off to Edinburg, Scotland, where they live. The gentleman worked on an oil rig way up north and was gone several months of the year away from family. We also had some great conversations and plenty of riotous laughter as well as "Lulabell" was returning from a visit with her boyfriend. Lulabell was seventy-six and traveling alone too. God bless her!

When we finally pulled into the train station, in Newcastle, I then had to find my way to the underground tube, now known as metro, to get to my destination, Tynemouth. That was an interesting ride, and, boy oh boy, did I have to hold on tight! I'm here. I did it. I stepped off the platform into a totally empty vast terminal room with not one person in sight. I tried to locate the bus, Uber, and taxi stands. Nothing. For the first time, I was a little dismayed at my circumstances. What do I do now? I stopped, and I prayed.

Then I walked a bit more, and there in the corner was a tiny pub that appeared to be closed. I tried the door, and it was open!

Thank You, Lord, for pubs! The bartender was washing up to close; there was one couple engrossed in each other in the corner, and I stated my case. This angel in disguise said, "No problem, ma'am. I'll call you a taxi." He did while pouring me a small ale on the house. "Ten minutes, love."

Ten minutes later, I was in the cab and headed to the Tynemouth Castle Inn.

As I ascended the stairs to the main lobby and opened the door, greeting me was a fully decorated Christmas tree, one of many I would discover. My oh my, what a wonderful hotel. This hotel had been closed for many years, I discovered, and just had its reopening two weeks prior to my arrival. This establishment was built in the roaring 1920s, so I'm told. It is Art Deco through and through. The exterior facade is bright white, curvy, sleek, strong, and classy. The interior is incredibly warm and inviting and again very classy. I feel luxury-laden.

I checked in and went upstairs to my room, the first one to stay in this room, and it was peaceful. I looked out my window, and right there looking back at me was the North Sea and Tynemouth.

I made it. By now I was so hungry and thirsty, having had nothing to eat all day.

I quickly freshened up and headed down to dinner.

You choose a table, check the menu and your table number, and head to the bar and order. Very common. I got a glass of hearty red from Australia and headed back to my table where I met the nicest couple who had their wedding reception here many years ago. They reminisced with me, enjoying the conversation. My fish dinner fresh from the sea was gobbled up pronto. When I had finished, I said my goodbyes, wished them many more years of happiness, and returned to my room. PJ's on, in a cozy bed, and thanking God for yet another safe journey and incredible blessings.

November 21, 2023
Tuesday

I woke early, showered, dressed, and headed downstairs for another included full breakfast. I was so excited to greet this lovely day and walk into Tynemouth. Tynemouth sits on the River Tyne and the North Sea. As I walked, I couldn't help but notice all the flowering fauna, including palm trees and bushes of various sizes. The sea air keeps everything in bloom, roses that smell like roses, rhododendron, and so many others.

It's November, I kept telling myself. It's approximately two miles into the heart of the village, which was where I first saw the Presbyterian Church.

I was sure it would give me some information. Sadly, after I took many photos of its dark exterior, I went inside to find it was no longer used as a church. No, what, really? A tattoo parlor and various other businesses inhabited this former home of residents' worship. I had to keep exploring and asking questions, which I did. Believe it or not, I went to the local liquor store, local since there was only one. The shop owner once told of my quest and stated, "Oh, one of the ladies who works here knows people from that church. She'll be in tomorrow."

So tomorrow I'll be back. I finished my walk completely around the town, passing by King George III Castle, which has an immense moat all around it, blanketed by the sea. Unfortunately, I couldn't visit as it's only open on weekends in November. By the time I returned to the inn, I was ready for a cup of tea and a wee little nap.

Once rested, I headed in the opposite direction north to another church called St. George's of Cullercoats. It was about two miles away right on the coast, and it was the color of the sand on the beach, golden and stately—majestic, really. This church was built in the 1880s by a famous architect by the name of John Loughborough

Pearson. I was surprised to find the door open as the churches back home are locked. Imagine trusting residents to enter as they wish to pray, which I did. The silence was deafening as they say. So I talked to God out loud in my usual way until it hit me that I might be in the very church where family members were married or attended or possibly had a funeral service or two.

The Heslops have lived and died here in the Tynemouth area for hundreds of years. If I haven't mentioned it before now, my grandmother's maiden name was Heslop. They were a hearty lot of mostly coal miners who were born, lived, and died in the same area. And from the people I've met so far, who would ever want to leave this place?

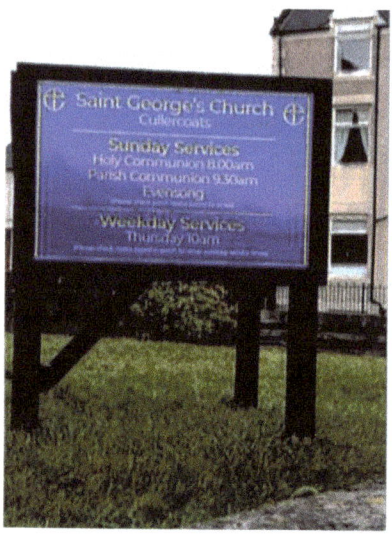

As I left the church and rounded the corner, I noticed a placard sign with service times at the front of the building. It noted the Sunday service, and beneath it, on Thursday, Parish Communion, 10:00 a.m. What? This Thursday is Thanksgiving in America, and I'm going to give thanks and attend! I walked back slowly to the inn as I was tired after walking fifteen thousand steps today according to my Fitbit. Yes, tonight I had a delicious dinner and, this time, two glasses of wine and went promptly to bed!

CONSTANT COMPANION

November 22, 2023
Wednesday

Awake, refreshed, and ready to go…where, I was not sure. I had another delightful breakfast to sustain whatever this day might bring. As I was contemplating my waitress, Deborah, who by now—as did many of the staff—knew of my trek to find my little Albert Edward, said, "Oh, Susan, you must take the 306 bus to Newcastle. The library with all kinds of historic records is there. Surely, they can help you." Someone else came to say good morning and suggested the same with a walk to Preston Cemetery first.

So without further ado, off I went. It was another pleasant day with sunshine intermittently, nice for today's adventure. It took fifteen minutes of walking to reach the cemetery. I entered, and someone greeted me asking "How can I help?" I gave her the information I was looking for, but alas, no Heslop of any spellings were found. She saw my disappointment and suggested I go to the Newcastle library. Once again, just hop on the 306! I was pointed in the right direction, and off I went.

When I arrived at the bus stop, I had no idea which direction was Newcastle; however, before long, a nice chap came to also take the bus, and he assured me this was the correct place and that the bus would stop at the terminal, last stop. A few minutes later, the now famous 306 arrived. Yes, it was two tiered and red, and I hopped aboard and took the only seat available on the main level. As God would have it, I sat next to Veronica.

Veronica and I are about the same in age, and she was very spunky, shall I say? Determined and self-reliant, yes; we would be friends. She asked why I was here, and of course, I told her. Her reply was "I want to help you with your trek. I'll show you how and take you to the library. It would be my pleasure."

I agreed only if I could treat her to tea. She finally agreed, and to the library we went. She was so patient and busied herself while I communicated to the staff, several staff who were now also on the hunt for little Albert Edward. We were beginning to lose hope when one of the gals said, "Wait a minute, I've found him!" She printed out the information I was searching for, and now I was, I was, I was lost for words.

My first uncle Albert Edward Heslop, who was born in 1901 in Northern Ireland to my grandmother and was moved by family to England, where he died in Blyth on Christmas Day 1903, age two, succumbing to pneumonia caused from whooping cough. Of course, I cried.

Veronica and I went to tea in a very cool bookstore. What a dear woman. After tea, we shopped a while in a beautiful shop where she had to return something for her granddaughter, which was the wrong size. A wonderful distraction to my mind after our collective discovery at the library. We headed back to the bus station and just made it on time, which was the last of the day. Phew. My new friend was not on the Internet, nor did she own a cell phone; however, she did give me her address and phone number. I hope we keep in touch with each other. I will do my part.

I hoped off at my stop in Tynemouth and decided to walk another route from the top of the hill on my way back to the inn. Suddenly, I saw a man who lost his footing and went down face-first to the ground. Another woman was coming from the opposite direction. She immediately started to ask him if he was alright and turned him over onto his back. This was when my nursing kicked in. I got down on the ground and told them who I was and to immediately call 911, and I assessed he had quite a gash on his face and his pulse was racing. Mine would be too! Yet he was quite elderly and used a cane, and I didn't know if he had broken a hip. The emergency call was made, and they said it would be about an hour. An hour! You are kidding me, right? It was cold, and he was on the ground bleeding! Another woman arrived and asked if there was anything she could do, and I asked if she lived nearby, which she did, and if she could get an old blanket or anything warm to cover him. She was back in a flash, and we covered him up, and I put his gloves back on to help keep his hands warm.

Now a gentleman came by, and he volunteered to go to his home to inform his wife what had happened and that he would be going to the local hospital once the ambulance arrived for full assessment and probably x-rays. Off he went. These people were incredible. So with a full brigade now on hand, I made my exit as it was nearly dark, and I had a steep hill to descend on a craggy road. As I walked, I intently minded my steps, hearing my mother in my head saying, "Oh, Suzy, be careful." I did stop occasionally to look up and view the sea from so high above, and it was breathtaking. I spotted a few ships with their twinkling lights in the distance.

Nearly there, and then I was back to the comfort of the inn.

I went directly to the bar and ordered a glass of French wine and took it to my room, where I changed my dirty clothes and freshened up. I'm so tired, but hunger won out. I had yet another delicious meal and dessert too. Please, now may someone point me to my bed?

Thank You, Lord, for this day to explore and find Albert Edward, for a new friend Veronica, and to assist and pray with a gentleman who knows You. May he be alright.

November 23, 2023
Thursday

Again I was up and ready to go. Breakfast was light today as I was headed off to St. George's Church for parish communion service at 10:00 a.m. I was the first one to arrive, so I sat in the front row.

Why not? A few minutes later, a gentleman came past me and turned to see who I was. He smiled but also had the quizzical look on his face as if to say, "Who are you? I don't recognize your face." He said nothing and arranged a few items on the altar and slipped behind somewhere and came back with his vestments on. By then, several others showed up, which when we exchanged "Peace be with you," I counted to seven.

The short but very poignant message went directly to my heart. This was Thanksgiving even though it was not celebrated here in the United Kingdom. I was given communion and thanked God for this vicar. When the quick but lovely service was over, the vicar came to me and said, "Would you like to join us at the vicarage for tea or coffee?"

"Oh, yes, please."

And off we went across the street. So by now, the curious congregation wanted to know why I was here, how did I get here, etc. I gave a brief tutorial of information. Now they were full of suggestions to find where Albert Edward might have been laid to rest, and I wrote them down.

The vicar said, "Shall we pray, and is there anything else we should pray for?"

Indeed, there was but not to be mentioned here. Everyone held out their hands, and we held on to each other and prayed. Simply divine.

I was anxious to get back to Tynemouth village and see if I could chat with the gal at the liquor store about the local church. She was there, and after we spoke, she couldn't offer any new information other than she knew people who used to attend years ago, but they had all passed. She never heard of the Heslops. Ah, well. I had heard or read somewhere that due to the climate change in France becoming too wet and warm for the champagne grapes, some vines, don't quote me, were transplanted to England as it is approximately ten degrees cooler than France. I inquired if they had ever heard about a new champagne, like bubbly, and they had it! It was twenty pounds and a small bottle, but I went for it as a gift to Mandy and John for their hospitality. I walked the long way back past the castle of King George III but just sat periodically and admired the astonishing views. I knew they would be my last, possibly.

After fifteen thousand steps this day, I dragged myself back to the inn, sat down, had wine, and you're right, yet another phenomenal meal with dessert. Then off to bed for me. I can't thank the Lord enough for this blessed Thanksgiving Day.

November 24, 2023
Friday

A train travel day back to Poole Harbor. I admit it, I fell in love with this area and more precisely the people I had come to meet and some of whom I can now call friends. I thank every one of you for joining my journey. I shall not soon forget your love and encouragement. As I was checking out, I asked Jason, the manager, to call me a cab or Uber ride. He tried, but he had some difficulty reaching someone. There was a couple having coffee nearby with their dog under the table who overheard our conversation.

The woman spoke first and said, "Oh, my husband can take you to the tube. It's just around the corner."

I said, "Oh, thank you, but no."

He stood up and said, "Come on then. Let's go, it's no trouble."

So I figured he was safe enough, having a wife and dog and all. Now at the tube station, I had to reverse in my mind the way I came to get back to Poole Harbor! Suzy did remember and am thanking myself very much. At one point, I had to disembark and wait and change to another train; an apparent tree was down across the tracks up ahead. So we all waited; it was cold, but there was a shelter, and I went in and sat down to wait for the replacement train. A mother and her baby, say two years of age, in her pram was watching something on the mom's cell phone. Mom was smoking some weed; lovely, right? Then the cell phone rang, and Mom pulled the phone out of her daughter's hand to answer, and baby had an utter and complete screaming meltdown tantrum. Mom gave the phone back to her, and now all was well. Wow, that was a lesson in how to not parent. She then lit another smoke. Incredulous. Yes, I suppose I was judging. Sorry, Lord, bless them both.

Back on the train. It was now delayed about twenty minutes, so I texted Mandy. Then she said, "We have been invited to Belfast tomorrow for the weekend, do you want to go?" My answer was "Why not?" I made yet another transfer in London and continued onto this new train until there was yet another delay of about twenty minutes going into Southampton. Congestion, they say, back up. I guess it wouldn't hurt to mention the rumors of another possible rail strike, citing lack of help, low wages, benefits. All the likely suspects I've heard in America before. All went okay after that. By the time I was back in Poole, it was late. Once again, my dear friend Mandy was waiting for me, and she said, if it's okay, we'll just have some leftovers tonight, which was more than fine with me. I was knackered, or the new slang is shattered, as they say, from a long day of sitting. I washed my clothes and lightly packed, and we were both in bed by 9:00 p.m. as we had to be up very early. Thank You, Lord, for this day. It was interesting to say the very least.

November 25, 2023
Saturday

    It was still dark when we got in the car to head for Southampton Airport for our very early flight to Belfast. It's only about an hour's drive from Poole Harbor, so we arrived in enough time to enjoy a coffee and light breakfast before our flight on Ryan Air. It had been a while since I flew on such a tiny plane, enough so that they had to ask a couple of passengers to change their seats for weight distribution—a bit disconcerting I must say. The stewardess, Heather, astounded me as she was dressed so professional, crisp, and said, "Welcome aboard, miss." It was so refreshing, and she reminded me of some of my air flights earlier in my life where the stewardesses dressed and served their passengers like they were special, and we had a nice chat after I complimented her. She asked, of course, where I was from, and we had a connection. Sweet blessings to each other.

    The flight was short and uneventful, just the way I like them. Finally, I was in Belfast! Well, truthfully, I drove here from Carrick on Shannon, Ireland, back in 2016 where I had rented a home. However, when I got to the huge roundabout on a steep incline, and I was alone sitting on the wrong side of the car on the wrong side of the road, I came to my natural senses and turned the car around. I was also close to Belfast when I drove from Dublin to North Ireland to see where my grandmother was born back in 1995 during the time of the Troubles, but that is another long, interesting story for another time. Not for any benefit to you, dear readers, but I did become an Irish citizen through my grandfather Flannigan from county Mayo. Ah, but that's also another story, dear reader.

    Mandy's daughter, Laura, picked us up and drove us back to her home to meet her husband, Emon, and their dog, Milo. I took an instant liking to Emon; he and Laura seemed to be a very good match. Milo has been trained very well from a young age. He's a smooth-haired black Labrador. As we were all getting to know one another, Milo came up to me as I was standing looking at the beautiful view and suddenly launched toward me full stance and yet instantly sat back on his haunches and never touched me. I was a bit stunned until Laura said, "Aw, he's doing the bunny for you!" He literally was sitting on his back legs with his two paws flopped in front, just like a bunny. That took a lot of training. I loved this sweet dog.

What a beautiful home they built, high and overlooking the River Lagan, where the *Titanic* was manufactured and launched. Once settled and bags dropped, tea and freshening up, we were off to downtown Belfast. I still am pinching myself that I am finally officially here! Emon dropped Mandy and me off a short distance to walk to the Crown, the oldest pub in Belfast. It was amazingly stunning with hand-carved dark wood from long ago, a totally unique tiled floor and bar, warm and fully friendly staff. It was packed at noontime with all sorts of revelers, yet we found a small pub table with two stools, and we grabbed it. Eventually, we found a third stool as Laura was going to meet us here for lunch. So we ordered a small Guiness, and I couldn't get the grin off my face. Someone dropped a full glass of beer onto the tile floor, and it made a loud bouncing banging sound, and when it settled without breaking, the entire crowd erupted into thundering applause. Yup, I'm here. We ordered lunch for ourselves, and Laura showed in time. After a second glass of Guiness and my treating to our amazing food and drink, we were off to the Christmas Market, just a short walking distance away.

The market was crowded with more revelers and shoppers. A typical outside marketplace I'd say but with Irish/British specialties. I didn't purchase a thing, not that I wasn't tempted, but I did have to carry the suitcase on my own back home. It was enjoyable to wander and observe it all. The market was directly in front of the city hall, so we decided to go into the very beautiful building mostly for my benefit. You see, John, Mandy's husband, grew up in Belfast and has lived through it all here. The good, the bad, and the ugly. Mandy also lived and worked here during the Troubles. This gorgeous, stately large, three-story-high white structure, rectangular in construction, is steeped in history to say the least. As we approached the stairs, we all observed a band warming up their instruments. They were a bit of a motley crew. By the time we ascended the stairs, there were numerous people coming out of the hall. It appeared someone had just gotten married! I said to my friend, "I'm waiting for the bride to come out." That's when she said, "Oh, do you see the woman in the white suit, she's the bride, and see the woman in the blue suit, she's her wife." Oh, okay, silly me. The band started to play, and they danced happily. Another first for me.

At this point, we were able to go inside, and what a tour we took throughout the building. It was so much information to consider. Basically, Belfast now has a three-tiered system of government, which is still not confirmed by the United Kingdom. The current lord mayor, Councilor Ryan Murphy, was elected June 5, 2023; he represents Sinn Fein. Next is deputy lord mayor, a female named Aine Groogan, who represents the Green Party. Lastly Councilor John Kyle, appointed January 18, 2023, and he represents the Ulster Unionist Party. And that, my dear readers, are all the politics you will get from me other than to say the now king of England has told them to get a government together or he will.

Continuing down the Main Street, Laura and Mandy pointed out the most bombed-out building. We won't go there. The Europa Hotel Belfast, the Grand Opera House, the Scottish Provident (for a little levity, a sign underneath stated Pizza on the Square, Donegall, which is where my grandmother Minnie Heslip was born), and many more sites of interest. Sooner or later, one must try and digest what has transpired over so many years in this city in North Ireland of which only one part is the feud against the Catholics and Protestants, those who want to remain loyal to the United Kingdom, and those who want a United Ireland.

We then went back to Laura and Emon and Milo's home. The lights were twinkling along the harbor. Time for a little rest and relaxation and laughter and just getting to know one another better. It was a marvelous evening together. Bedtime was early as they had another day planned for tomorrow. Thank You, Lord, that I finally was able to experience this wonderful place and its lovely people.

CONSTANT COMPANION

November 26, 2023
Sunday

    We were all awake early, dressed, and ready for another adventure. I was offered tea and toasted homemade bread, which was delicious. Milo greeted me with a soft woof and a kiss. The four of us were going to the Titanic Museum followed by high tea at the Titanic Hotel afterward. Within minutes, we arrived and went in as previous tickets were purchased and presented at the entrance. My first impression was that this structure had been very carefully thought out and designed to honor the men who in this very spot built the forever known—is there anyone ever who has not heard of it?—*Titanic*! I struggled for a time wondering if I could even write anything about this experience. Truly, it was an emotional three hours. I've decided to briefly mention the company Harland & Wolf Ltd. that had designed and built the ship on this very spot and saw her launched. On an uncanny note, she was launched between Spencer Dock and Albert Dock. This museum tells the story of the fifteen thousand men who built her and the many hours of their intense toil as well as the heart-wrenching tale of her demise. This is a solemn place that must be experienced on one's own if possible. April 10, 1912, was her maiden and only voyage.

    When we had completed our tour, I purchased a third-class teacup for remembrance. Across from the museum was the Titanic Hotel Belfast, where we had reservations at twelve for afternoon tea. We had our choice of seven different teas, and I chose the Single Estate Darjeeling, which is described as grown in the foothills of the Himalayas, sourced from prize-winning single-estate Bannockburn leaves known as the champagne of teas. Now onto the menu. We had two three-tiered gold serving plates. One was vegan for Mandy and Laura, and the other Emon and I shared. On the bottom plate were a selection of delicate gourmet sandwiches; in the middle plate were scones, clotted cream, butter, and jams; and crowning the top tier were several sweet treats, many of which were topped with fresh berries. No, we couldn't finish it all and took some home with us!

On the way home, there was a stop at the corner store for milk, and I found the Irwin's Wheaten bread I so loved when I was last in Ireland. I bought myself a loaf and was determined to pack it into my suitcase. Another sidenote: Emon and Laura were married and had their wedding reception at this extravagant hotel, which previously was the offices of H&W. They gave me a tour of the place, which included the preserved room where the architects designed the *Titanic*.

Once back at the house, Laura and I took Milo for a walk. The night was more about getting to know each other better, the work they do, plans, and the like. They met at Queens University Belfast (QUB), which received its charter in 1845 and is a public research university. We had an interesting conversation regarding AI and how it may affect all our futures. Now off to bed for Mandy and me since we have an early flight back to England.

Thank You so much, Lord, not meaning to sound repetitive; however, this I indeed know: I am truly blessed.

November 27, 2023
Monday

We were dropped off at the airport for our flight to Southampton. The airport was decorated in Christmas lights, with a huge tree in the lobby. Laura was off to work and had to leave us, but it gave us plenty of time to check in and have some breakfast and a coffee before our flight. Once back in Southampton, the drive back to Highfield House in Poole looked inviting, including my little room under the stairs. John was home from where he worked in Liverpool and had put up the Christmas tree and decorated it in the living room, along with all the other holiday decorations. Wow, what a nice surprise for us both.

I washed and dried my clothes (only three outfits—did I tell you I pack light?—plus the outfit I was wearing) again and packed. A second surprise from John when he knew I had special papers to store, he gifted me a treasure box that he made himself with a painting of Corfe Castle in Dorset, which I have been to three times, hand-painted in the top center of the wooden box. It fits perfectly all my papers, and I will love it forever to store my heritage papers when I return home to America. John's third surprise was giving me a personal signed copy of his latest book, *A Ballad of Beliefs: The Complete Trilogy* by John McCormick. John had previously written three separate books about the times during 1989 and 1990, which I thoroughly enjoyed a couple of years ago. They're about growing up in troubled Belfast, *Crawl*, *Rise*, and *Race*, which I very highly recommend.

The fourth surprise: "I'm treating you to a nice farewell dinner out tonight. So get a quick rest, and then we'll be off."

So I think the fifth surprise was the most enlightening. John heard my story telling about the first trek to Swallowfield and finding the church. He sat there smiling and said, "You've got a good book there."

"Oh, no," was my reply.

He again simply stated, "Write it down. People will be interested."

So I am writing it down.

We went to Mandy's favorite spot for a cocktail first, and she enjoyed showing me around. The food was Thai, and the decor made me think I was in Thailand. She had ordered takeaway from here my first night in town, and it was tastefully exotic, but they were fully booked tonight. So we walked a little way to another restaurant and had a delightful bottle of wine, which they finally relented I could treat us to. The dinner was an amazing, delicious last supper together.

November 28, 2023
Tuesday

I hate long goodbyes, always preferring to say, "See you when I see you, friends." I am homeward bound now to America on the coach from Poole Harbor for three hours to London Heathrow. I reminisced and cried some, not knowing when or if I would ever return.

Thank You, Lord, for being my constant companion.

About the Author

Mary Susan Spencer Cuminale resided most of her life in Rochester, New York. She lived through the '60s—with the assassinations of JFK, Robert Kennedy, and Martin Luther King Jr. and the Vietnam War. Married in 1969, she had two beautiful children and devoted herself to them. After twenty-five years, she divorced and learned over time to become who she is today. She is a loyal friend with a passion for travel and adventure.

www.ingramcontent.com/pod-product-compliance
Lightning Source LLC
LaVergne TN
LVHW060324220125
801850LV00001B/2